# SESAME STREET

# Explore
# RAIN FOREST
# HABITATS
## with Abby

Charlotte Reed

Lerner Publications ◆ Minneapolis

# There are many habitats to explore!

In the Sesame Street® Habitats series, young readers will take a tour of eight habitats. Join your friends from *Sesame Street* as they learn about these different habitats where animals live, sleep, and find food and water.

Sincerely,
The Editors at Sesame Workshop

# Table of Contents

# WHAT IS A HABITAT?

Let's explore habitats! A habitat is a place where animals live and can find water, food, and a place to sleep. A rain forest is a type of habitat.

Many different animals live in a rain forest!

A rain forest has many trees and gets a lot of rain. There are many, many kinds of plants in rain forests.

These trees are much taller than me!

# LET'S LOOK AT RAIN FOREST HABITATS

In a rain forest, the tree leaves often block the sun. This makes the forest floor shady and warm. Smaller trees and plants grow in the spots of sunlight that shine through the treetops.

Plants need sun to grow.

This toucan flies high above the trees.
It has a large, colorful beak that helps it
pick and eat fruit.

Lemurs live in rain forest trees. Their tails help them balance as they leap from tree to tree to find fruit and leaves to eat.

Ring-tailed lemurs eat leaves from tamarind trees!

Sloths spend most of their time in trees. They eat and sleep while hanging from branches. Sloths move very slowly on land.

They might be slow on land, but sloths are very fast swimmers!

15

Some animals, like okapis, live on the ground of a rainforest. Okapis are herbivores. That means they only eat plants.

Okapis find all of their food on the forest floor and on branches.

This anteater also lives in the rain forest.
Anteaters eat different kinds of insects like
ants and termites.

The anteater's tongue helps it eat insects.

Some animals can blend in with the trees and plants of the rain forest. This is called camouflage.

Camouflage makes it hard to see some animals!

This jaguar is camouflaged. Jaguars have spots that help them blend into the trees and grass around them.

Can you SPOT the jaguar?

Blue morpho butterflies
have bright blue wings!

When they close their wings, their underside is a brown color that helps them blend into the tree bark.

Butterflies are beautiful!

There are so many interesting animals in the rain forest! Which is your favorite?

It's hard to choose just one!

# 1. Which of these pictures is of a rain forest habitat?

A

B

## 2. Which of these animals lives in a rain forest habitat?

A

B

# Glossary

**beak:** a part of a bird's mouth

**camouflage:** to blend in with one's surroundings

**habitat:** a place where animals live and can find water, food, and a place to sleep

**herbivores:** animals that only eat plants

# Can You Guess? Answers

1. A
2. A

# Read More

Peters, Katie. *Under the Rain Forest Canopy*. Minneapolis: Lerner Publications, 2020.

Reed, Charlotte. *Explore Grassland Habitats with Ji-Young*. Minneapolis: Lerner Publications, 2024.

Sabelko, Rebecca. *Rain Forest Animals*. Minneapolis: Bellwether Media, 2023.

# Photo Acknowledgments

Images used: Ethan Daniels/Shutterstock, p. 1; SimonSkafar/Getty Images, p. 5; kiszon pascal/Getty Images, p. 6; Zairo/Shutterstock, p. 9; Fernando Calmon/Shutterstock, p. 10; Steve Taylor ARPS/Alamy, p. 11; blickwinkel/Alamy, p. 12; Zoonar GmbH/Alamy, p.13; kjorgen/Getty Images, p. 14; Gleb_Ivanov/Getty Images, p. 16; Juniors Bildarchiv GmbH/Alamy, p. 17; Pablo Rodriguez Merkel/Shutterstock, p. 18; David Havel/Alamy, p. 19; dennisvdw/Getty Images, pp. 20, 21; Theo Allofs/Getty Images, p. 23; Haitong Yu/Getty Images, p. 24; Maximilian Andre/Shutterstock, p. 25; Paul S. Wolf/Shutterstock (bottom left), p. 26; agefotostock/Alamy (spread), p. 26; Kung_Mangkorn/Getty Images, p. 27; Ian Beattle/Alamy (left), p. 28; Bill Gorum/Alamy (right), p. 28; Joe Hendrickson/Getty Images (left), p. 29; Andrew Lawlor/500px/Getty Images (right), p. 29.
Cover: Zoonar GmbH/Alamy; Mats Lindberg/Alamy; Wild-Places/Getty Images; nodrama_llama/Shutterstock.

# Index

For the Cole family and our many travels, memories, and laughs together.

Lerner Publications Company
An imprint of Lerner Publishing Group, Inc.
241 First Avenue North
Minneapolis, MN 55401 USA

For reading levels and more information, look up this title at www.lernerbooks.com.

Main body text set in Mikado provided by HVD.

**Library of Congress Cataloging-in-Publication Data**

Names: Reed, Charlotte, 1997– author.
Title: Explore rain forest habitats with Abby / Charlotte Reed.
Description: Minneapolis : Lerner Publications, [2024] | Series: Sesame Street habitats | Includes bibliographical references and index. | Audience: Ages 4–8 | Audience: Grades K–1 | Summary: "From the tops of the trees to the forest's floor, the rain forest is an amazing habitat. Learn more about rain forest animals with Abby and the rest of the friends from Sesame Street"– Provided by publisher.
Identifiers: LCCN 2023004525 (print) | LCCN 2023004526 (ebook) | ISBN 9798765604229 (lib. bdg.) | ISBN 9798765617700 (epub)
Subjects: LCSH: Rain forest animals—Habitations—Juvenile literature. | Rain forest ecology—Juvenile literature. | BISAC: JUVENILE NONFICTION / Science & Nature / Environmental Science & Ecosystems
Classification: LCC QL112 .R445 2024 (print) | LCC QL112 (ebook) | DDC 591.734—dc23/eng/20230420

LC record available at https://lccn.loc.gov/2023004525
LC ebook record available at https://lccn.loc.gov/2023004526

ISBN 979-8-7656-2490-6 (pbk.)

Manufactured in the United States of America
1-1009559-51409-5/30/2023